Senior Year Head Start

for

9th, 10th and 11th Grade

Also by Marianne Ragins

Winning Scholarships for College
College Survival & Success Skills 101

Senior Year

Head Start

for

9th, 10th and 11th Grade

Get money for college before your high school senior year!

Marianne Ragins

TSW Publishing
P. O. Box 176
Centreville, Virginia 20122
www.scholarshipworkshop.com
TSW Publishing is a division of The Scholarship Workshop LLC

Copyright © 2016, 2019 by Marianne Ragins
All rights reserved. No part of this book may be used or reproduced in any manner whatsoever without prior written consent of the author, except as provided by the United States of America copyright law.

Senior Year Head Start was written to provide accurate advice to readers. However, please note that the author nor the publisher are engaged in the practice of providing legal, accounting, tax or other professional advice unless otherwise indicated. If you need legal, accounting, tax or other advice, please consult a professional in the appropriate area. Neither the author, the publisher, nor any entity associated with *Senior Year Head Start* assume any liability for errors, omissions, or inaccuracies. Any action you take or do not take as a result of reading *Senior Year Head Start* is entirely your responsibility.

ISBN: 978-0-9767660-9-4

Printed in the United States of America

This book is available at special quantity discounts for bulk purchases for sales promotions, premiums, fundraising, and educational use. Special versions or book excerpts can also be created to fit specific needs.

For more information, please contact info@scholarshipworkshop.com or call 703 579-4245. You can also write: TSW Publishing, P. O. Box 176, Centreville, Virginia 20122.

Dedication

To my mother, my husband and my little ones; your love, motivation, and presence in my life keep me going.

For G. L. Solomon
As one who truly got the most from life
and helped us to get the most from ours,
your sunny smile, loving heart and
generous ways will be remembered forever
by all of your family and friends.

CONTENTS

Introduction 11
Scholarship Programs for Young Students 14
    Elementary School 14
    Middle School Only 22
    Middle and High School 25
Can Graduating from High School Early Affect Your Scholarship Chances? 44
Are Scholarships Available for Private School? 46
Scholarships as a Younger Student Versus a High School Senior 47
    What's the Difference? 47
    What's the Same? 47
The Search 49
    Library Search 49
    Internet Search 50
    Advanced Internet Search 50
    Using General Search Engines 52
    Local Search 53
Applications 57
Winning Elements 59

    Your résumé/activity list 59

    Essays 59

    Samples of your work 60

    Articles..61

    Recommendations 62

    Résumé/Activity List 62

    Recommendations 64

The Essay 67

Application Checklist...74

Keys to Preparing for College in High School..............78

Other Resources from Marianne Ragins 82

    Books and Publications 82

    Workshops & Boot Camps.....................................83

    Webinars & Online Classes....................................85

About the Author..86

Introduction

Can you imagine having a scholarship or an award won before you become a high school senior? This could mean extra freedom for you when you do reach the pinnacle, your final year of high school. Then you could devote all of your time to being a senior and focusing on your dream college or university. Of course, scholarships and awards change every year but currently there are scholarships and awards you can win as early as age 6, particularly if you have already started volunteering and helping out in the community.

Scholarships and money available for younger students especially for those not yet in high school is often associated with prize winnings for art, writing, speaking or other talent contests such as the *American Legion National High School Oratorical Contest* and the *Doodle 4 Google* contest. Or the money is associated with outstanding community service such as the *Jesse Brown Memorial Youth Scholarship Program*. Too, there are scholarships associated with recognizing exceptional talent or scientific interests early, such as the *Davidson Fellows Scholarship*.

If you're a parent reading this publication and you're grooming your son or daughter to have the best chances of getting scholarship or prize money to help with college early, encourage them to explore their creative and scientific side. Also help them to understand the importance of giving back. A focus on both will boost their opportunities for scholarships as a young student but also for scholarships as high school senior. In addition, it will help improve their applications for entrance into competitive colleges and universities.

Middle class students with little or no need will also benefit from participating in community service and exploration into potential special talents. Many of the scholarships and awards for younger students have no financial need requirements.

If you win a scholarship before you actually start your college studies, the money is usually held for you by the sponsoring organization. Once you notify the organization with information about your college or university, funds are often dispersed directly to the school. There are some awards you can win that are not technically considered scholarships and the funds may be sent directly to you immediately after you win. This information is normally included in the sponsor's program materials or website. If funds are remitted directly to you, save! Don't spend! Or, if necessary, the funds could be spent to help pay for a current year's private school tuition, if you believe the benefits of the money being used for private school now outweigh the benefits of helping to pay for college later.

Introduction

To help give you a jumpstart on money you can win before your 12th grade year, the following chapter includes a list of opportunities you can start pursuing even before you leave kindergarten or branch out from middle school.

1

Scholarship Programs for Young Students

The following awards and scholarships are general. They can be used for most majors and career fields and a variety of students are eligible to apply for them. Please contact each organization to confirm or update deadlines and eligibility criteria. Under no circumstances should you use this listing as the sole resource for your scholarship search. The purpose of this publication is to help you find scholarships that are specific to your situation and to show you steps to help you win them. The provision of the following list of scholarships is meant only to give you a jump-start on the scholarship process.

Elementary School

Caring Awards

Caring Institute
228 7th Street SE
Washington, DC 20003
(202) 547-4273
E-mail: info@caring.org
Website: http://www.caring.org

1 – Scholarship Programs for Young Students

Social Media: Follow Caring Institute on Twitter (@CaringOrg)
Additional Information: If you haven't yet graduated from high school or reached your eighteenth birthday, you can be nominated for a Caring Award from the Caring Institute if you've been deeply involved in activities that show your depth of caring for your community, state, region, or the world. Winners of this award are considered role models with an extraordinary sense of public service. Past winners have received this award for activities such as founding organizations designed to serve others and/or making a meaningful impact in their high school, community, state, or beyond.

Davidson Fellows Scholarship

Davidson Institute for Talent Development
(775) 852-3483 ext. 435
E-mail: DavidsonFellows@davidsongifted.org
Website: http://www.davidsongifted.org/fellows or http://www.davidson fellows.org
Social Media: Follow DavidsonGifted on Facebook (https://www.facebook.com/DavidsonGifted and Twitter (@DavidsonGifted)
Additional Information: The Davidson Fellows scholarships range from $10,000 to $50,000 for students age 18 and under who have completed a significant piece of work. The program looks for students whose projects are at, or close to, the

college-graduate level with a depth of knowledge in their particular area of study. The application categories are Science, Technology, Engineering, Mathematics, Literature, Music, Philosophy, and Outside the Box. To apply you must be a U.S. citizen or a permanent resident residing in the United States, or be stationed overseas due to active U.S. military duty. There is no minimum age for eligibility. See website for specific details and guidelines for entering this competition.

Doodle 4 Google

Website: www.google.com/doodle4google
Additional Information: Doodle 4 Google is an annual program that encourages K-12 students in the United States to use their artistic talents to think big and redesign the Google homepage logo for millions to see. Previous themes have been "My Best Day Ever…" and "What I Want to Do Someday…" Winning student artists will see their artwork appear on the Google homepage, receive a $30,000 college scholarship, and a $50,000 technology grant for their school along with other prizes. Visit the website for complete eligibility guidelines, templates, and submission information.

1 – Scholarship Programs for Young Students

The Gloria Barron Prize for Young Heroes

P.O. Box 1470
Boulder, CO 80302
E-mail: admin@barronprize.org
Website: https://barronprize.org
Additional Information: Each year, the Gloria Barron Prize for Young Heroes honors outstanding youth leaders ages 8 to 18 who have made a significant positive difference to people and the environment. Top winners in this program receive a $10,000 cash award to support their service work or higher education. You must include a reference letter for this prize. The deadline is usually in April. Visit the website for additional information about references, application requirements and other details.

Jesse Brown Memorial Youth Scholarship Program

Disabled American Veterans
Voluntary Services Department
P.O. Box 14301
Cincinnati, OH 45250-0301
Website: http://www.dav.org (search *Jesse Brown Youth Memorial Scholarship*) or link to http://www.dav.org/volunteers/Scholarship.aspx

Senior Year Head Start

Additional Information: The Jesse Brown Memorial Youth Scholarship Program was established to recognize youth volunteers age 21 or younger who have volunteered for a minimum of 100 hours at a VA medical center during the previous calendar year. You must be nominated for this program and write a 750 word essay entitled "What Volunteering Has Meant to Me." You can also nominate yourself. See the website for additional eligibility criteria, current deadlines and the nomination form. Scholarship amounts can be up to $20,000.

Optimist International Oratorical Contest

Optimist International Headquarters
4494 Lindell Boulevard
St. Louis, MO 63108
(800) 500-8130 or (314) 371-6000
Email: programs@optimist.org
Website: http://www.optimist.org (click on *Home\Members\Scholarship Contests*)

Additional Information: This scholarship is based on your ability to prepare and present a four to five minute speech on a specific topic within a timed period. Contestants, who must be no more than 19 years of age at the time of contest entry, must speak about the official oratorical contest subject which changes each year. For example, one year's contest subject was, "Why My Voice is Important." Contest is open to citizens of the US, Canada and the Caribbean. You must enter the contest through your local Optimist Club. To get contact information for your local Optimist club, visit the website. Students must compete in several levels. Visit the website for more details. Award amounts range up to $2,500.

Author's Personal Note: I competed in the Optimist International Oratorical Contest for several years at various levels beginning in the sixth grade, usually winning at each level but not the final level. Although I did not win the $1,500 award available at that time, I did gain invaluable experience in public speaking and in writing speeches which also helped me to write essays. These are very important skills to have especially if you want to win scholarships. It will help you in both interviews (the ability to speak well in public) and in preparing essays.

Optimist International Essay Contest

Optimist International Headquarters
4494 Lindell Boulevard
St. Louis, MO 63108
(800) 500-8130 or (314) 371-6000
Email: programs@optimist.org
Website: http://www.optimist.org (click on *Home\Members\Scholarship Contests*)

Senior Year Head Start

Additional Information: This is a multi-level essay writing contest. Student winners at the district and international level win scholarships. Contestants must be no more than 19 years of age at the time of contest entry. Contest is open to citizens of the US, Canada and the Caribbean. You must enter the contest through your local Optimist Club. To get contact information for your local Optimist club, visit the website for more details.

Profile in Courage Essay Contest

Columbia Point
Boston, MA 02125
Website: www.jfklibrary.org
Additional Information: In recognition of one of President Kennedy's most important legacies, this contest is designed to promote the involvement of young people in the civic life of their country. High school students in the 9th through 12th grades can participate in this essay contest, by writing a compelling 1000 word (maximum) essay and citing at least five sources on the meaning of political courage. Registration forms must be submitted with the essay and are available on the website. The first place winner and the nominating teacher will be invited to receive awards at the Kennedy Library in Boston. Awards range from $500 to $10,000. The contest deadline is usually in early January of each year.

1 – Scholarship Programs for Young Students

The Prudential Spirit of Community Awards

Website: http://spirit.prudential.com
Additional Information: This program, sponsored by Prudential in partnership with the National Association of Secondary School Principals (NASSP), recognizes students in grades 5 – 12 who have demonstrated exemplary community service. Local honorees are selected at participating schools and organizations in November, and from these winners, two state honorees are chosen from each state and the District of Columbia. State honorees receive an award of $1,000, an engraved silver medallion, and an all-expenses-paid trip to Washington, D.C. National honorees receive an additional award of $5,000, an engraved gold medallion, a crystal trophy for their school or organization and a $5,000 grant from The Prudential Foundation for a non-profit, charitable organization of their choice. Although this program is not officially a scholarship, the funds you win, if you're an avid volunteer, could add nicely to the money in your college fund to pay for your educational expenses.

Scripps National Spelling Bee

Website: https://spellingbee.com
Social Media: Follow the Scripps National Spelling Bee on Facebook

Senior Year Head Start

(https://www.facebook.com/scrippsnationalspellingbee) and Twitter (@Scrippsbee)

Additional Information: The Scripps National Spelling Bee contest is open to elementary and middle school students who participate in the spelling bee competition. Student champions can win up to $40,000.

Sodexo Foundation

Stephen J. Brady STOP Hunger Scholarships
9801 Washingtonian Blvd.
Gaithersburg, MD 20878
Website:://us.stop-hunger.org/home.html or http://www.sodexofoundation.org (see *Grants and Scholarships*)
Additional Information: Stephen J. Brady STOP Hunger Scholarships are open to students in kindergarten through graduate school who are enrolled in an accredited educational institution in the United States. The scholarships are available to students who have performed unpaid volunteer services impacting hunger in a community within the United States at least within the last 12 months. Additional consideration is given to students working to fight childhood hunger. A Community Service Recommendation is required for this application form so ask recommenders (who must not be family members) for their recommendations early. For more on requesting recommendations, see chapter 13, "The Art of Getting Good

1 – Scholarship Programs for Young Students

Recommendations & Requesting Nominations" in *Winning Scholarships for College* (5th edition).

Middle School Only

Angela Award

National Science Teachers Association
1840 Wilson Boulevard
Arlington VA 22201
Website: www.nsta.org (search for Angela Award)
Additional Information: Female students in grades 5–8, who are involved in or have a strong connection to science, can be nominated for this award. The award was established in honor of Gerry Wheeler, Executive Director Emeritus, to recognize his outstanding dedication to the National Science Teachers Association and lifelong commitment to science education. The award is a $1,000 US EE Savings Bond or Canadian Savings Bond purchased for the equivalent issue price.

Mathcounts

Website: www.mathcounts.org
Additional Information: Mathcounts is a middle school series of programs that include a mathematics competition and a math video challenge contest. In the mathematics competition, students have a chance to win a $20,000 scholarship. In the video contest, students can win up to $1,000.

Senior Year Head Start

Patriot's Pen Competition

Veterans of Foreign Wars
National Headquarters & Ladies Auxiliary
406 West 34th St.
Kansas City, MO 64111
Website: www.vfw.org
Additional Information: Students must write an essay expressing their views on a patriotic theme that changes annually. The contest is sponsored by the Veterans of Foreign Wars Organization (VFW). Awards range from $500 to $5,000. The contest is open to students in grades 6 through 8.

Scripps National Spelling Bee

Website: https://spellingbee.com
Social Media: Follow the Scripps National Spelling Bee on Facebook (https://www.facebook.com/scrippsnationalspellingbee) and Twitter (@Scrippsbee)

Additional Information: The Scripps National Spelling Bee contest is open to elementary and middle school students who participate in the spelling bee competition. Student champions can win up to $40,000.

1 – Scholarship Programs for Young Students

Middle and High School

American Legion National High School Oratorical Contest

(317) 630-1200
E-mail: oratorical@legion.org
Website: http://www.legion.org (See *Programs\Family and Youth\Scholarships\Oratorical Contest*)

Additional Information: Open to students in grades 9 through 12 who are less than 20 years of age (as of the national contest deadline) and are U.S. citizens or lawful permanent residents of the United States. You must be currently enrolled in a high school or middle school (public, parochial, military, private, or state-accredited homeschool) in which the curriculum is considered to be of high school level. You must be able to prepare and deliver speeches in public to win these awards. In addition to the scholarships awarded by the national headquarters, several hundred scholarships may be awarded by intermediate organizations to participants at the post, district, county, or department levels of competition. Visit the website for more details and current deadlines. Award amounts range from $1,500 to $18,000.

Ayn Rand's Novelette Anthem Essay Contest

Website: www.aynrand.org/contests
Additional Information: Open to 8th, 9th and 10th grade high school students who submit an essay of 600 to 1200 words. Awards range from $30 to $2,000.

Ayn Rand's Novel The Fountainhead Essay Contest

Website: www.aynrand.org/contests
Additional Information: Open to 11th and 12th grade high school students who submit an essay of 800 to 1600 words. Awards range from $50 to $10,000.

C-Span's Student Cam

Website: http://www.studentcam.org
Additional Information: StudentCam is an annual national video documentary from C-SPAN that encourages students to think critically about issues that affect the nation and its communities. To enter this competition you must be in grades 6-12 and create a short (5-6 minute) video documentary on a topic related to the yearly competition theme. You can compete individually or in teams of either two or three members and your video documentary must include clips of supporting C-SPAN video

relating to the topic. Up to $100,000 in cash prizes are awarded.

Caring Awards

Caring Institute
228 7th Street SE
Washington, DC 20003
(202) 547-4273
E-mail: info@caring.org
Website: http://www.caring.org
Social Media: Follow Caring Institute on Twitter (@CaringOrg)
Additional Information: If you haven't yet graduated from high school or reached your eighteenth birthday, you can be nominated for a Caring Award from the Caring Institute if you've been deeply involved in activities that show your depth of caring for your community, state, region, or the world. Winners of this award are considered role models with an extraordinary sense of public service. Past winners have received this award for activities such as founding organizations designed to serve others and/or making a meaningful impact in their high school, community, state, or beyond.

College JumpStart Scholarship

c/o College JumpStart Scholarship Fund
4546 B10 El Camino Real No. 325

Senior Year Head Start

Los Altos, California 94022
Website: www.jumpstart-scholarship.net
Additional Information: This scholarship is open to 10th through 12th grade high school students, college students and non-traditional students who are U.S. citizens or legal residents. You must be attending or planning to attend an accredited 2-year, 4-year or vocational/trade school in the U.S. and be committed to using education to better your life and that of your family and/or community. Deadlines are normally in April and October.

Courage in Student Journalism Awards

Student Press Law Center
1101 Wilson Blvd., Suite 1100
Arlington, VA 22209
Website: http://www.kent.edu/csj/courage-student-journalism-awards or visit www.kent.edu and search for, *Courage in Student Journalism Awards*
Additional Information: Open to middle and high school students who have stood in support of the First Amendment. Deadlines are usually in June of each year. Students must be nominated but you can also nominate yourself. Awards are up to $1000. See website for additional details.

1 – Scholarship Programs for Young Students

Create-A-Greeting Card Scholarship Contest

Website: www.gallerycollection.com/greetingcardscontests.htm or www.gallerycollection.com/greeting-cards-scholarship.htm

Additional Information: This $10,000 scholarship contest is open to all high school AND college students AND members of the armed forces who are enrolled during the time-period of the contest in an academic program designed to conclude with the awarding of a diploma or a degree. To participate, applicants must create a design for a Christmas card, holiday card, birthday card or all-occasion greeting card. Legal residents of the fifty (50) United States, the District of Columbia, American Samoa, Guam, the Commonwealth of the Northern Mariana Islands, the U.S. Virgin Islands, and Puerto Rico are eligible to enter. International students who have a student visa to attend school in the United States are considered legal residents and are also eligible to enter.

Davidson Fellows Scholarship

Davidson Institute for Talent Development
(775) 852-3483 ext. 435
E-mail: DavidsonFellows@davidsongifted.org
Website: http://www.davidsongifted.org/fellows or http://www.davidsonfellows.org

Social Media: Follow DavidsonGifted on Facebook (https://www.facebook.com/DavidsonGifted and Twitter (@DavidsonGifted)

Additional Information: The Davidson Fellows scholarships range from $10,000 to $50,000 for students age 18 and under who have completed a significant piece of work. The program looks for students whose projects are at, or close to, the college-graduate level with a depth of knowledge in their particular area of study. The application categories are Science, Technology, Engineering, Mathematics, Literature, Music, Philosophy, and Outside the Box. To apply you must be a U.S. citizen or a permanent resident residing in the United States, or be stationed overseas due to active U.S. military duty. There is no minimum age for eligibility. See website for specific details and guidelines for entering this competition.

Doodle 4 Google

Website: www.google.com/doodle4google

Additional Information: Doodle 4 Google is an annual program that encourages K-12 students in the United States to use their artistic talents to think big and redesign the Google homepage logo for millions to see. Previous themes have been "My Best Day Ever…" and "What I Want to Do Someday…" Winning student artists will see their artwork appear on the Google homepage, receive a

1 – Scholarship Programs for Young Students

$30,000 college scholarship, and a $50,000 technology grant for their school along with other prizes. Visit the website for complete eligibility guidelines, templates, and submission information.

DoSomething.Org Easy Scholarship Campaigns

Website: http://www.dosomething.org (see Scholarships section on the website).
Social Media: Follow DoSomething.org on Facebook (https://www.facebook.com/dosomething) or Twitter (@dosomething)
Additional Information: DoSomething.org is a nonprofit for young people focused on social change for causes such as bullying, homelessness, and cancer. To apply for a scholarship, you need to complete a campaign and prove it with pictures of you in action during the campaign. They have many campaigns featured on the website. The scholarship program is open to U.S. and Canadian citizens 25 and under and does not require a minimum GPA. Winners are chosen through a random drawing.

The Gloria Barron Prize for Young Heroes

The Barron Prize

Senior Year Head Start

545 Pearl Street
Boulder, Colorado 80302
Website: www.barronprize.org
Additional Information: Each year, the Gloria Barron Prize for Young Heroes honors outstanding youth leaders ages 8 to 18 who have made a significant positive difference to people and our planet. Top winners in this program receive a $2,500 cash award to support their service work or higher education. You must be nominated for this prize. Visit the website for additional information about nominations, application requirements and other details.

Intel International Science and Engineering Fair (Intel ISEF)

Website: https://student.societyforscience.org

Additional Information: Students worldwide in grades 9 through 12 or equivalent compete in an Intel ISEF affiliated science fair to win the right to attend the Intel ISEF and earn up to $75,000 at Intel ISEF each year.

Jesse Brown Memorial Youth Scholarship Program

Disabled American Veterans
Voluntary Services Department
P.O. Box 14301

1 – Scholarship Programs for Young Students

Cincinnati, OH 45250-0301
Website: http://www.dav.org (search *Jesse Brown Youth Memorial Scholarship*) or link to http://www.dav.org/volunteers/Scholarship.aspx
Additional Information: The Jesse Brown Memorial Youth Scholarship Program was established to recognize youth volunteers age 21 or younger who have volunteered for a minimum of 100 hours at a DAV or DAV facility such as a VA medical center during the previous calendar year. You must be nominated for this program and write a 750-word essay titled "What Volunteering Has Meant to Me." You can also nominate yourself. See the website for additional eligibility criteria, current deadlines, and the nomination form. Scholarship amounts can be up to $20,000.

National Young Arts Foundation

Programs Department
2100 Biscayne Boulevard
Miami, FL 33137
(800) 970-ARTS
E-mail: info@youngarts.org
Website: http://www.ARTSawards.org or http://www.nfaa.org
Additional Information: This talent search competition is open to high school students between the ages of 15 and 18 (or in grades 10 through 12) with talent in the arts such as dance,

writing, music, theater, visual arts, and jazz. Awards can be used for any field of study. To apply, you must be a citizen or permanent resident of the United States or its official territories (e.g., Puerto Rico). The deadline for final submission is in October. There is an application fee for this program. See the website for details.

Optimist International Oratorical Contest

Optimist International Headquarters
4494 Lindell Boulevard
St. Louis, MO 63108
(800) 500-8130 or (314) 371-6000
Email: programs@optimist.org
Website: http://www.optimist.org (click on *Home\Members\Scholarship Contests*)

Additional Information: This scholarship is based on your ability to prepare and present a four to five minute speech on a specific topic within a timed period. Contestants, who must be no more than 19 years of age at the time of contest entry, must speak about the official oratorical contest subject which changes each year. For example, one year's contest subject was, "Why My Voice is Important." Contest is open to citizens of the US, Canada and the Caribbean. You must enter the contest through your local Optimist Club. To get contact information for your local Optimist club, visit the website for additional information. Students must compete in several levels. Visit the website for more details. Award amounts range up to $2,500. *Author's Personal Note:* I competed in the Optimist International Oratorical Contest for several years at various levels beginning in the sixth grade, usually winning at each level but not the final level. Although I did not win the $1,500 award available at that time, I did gain invaluable experience in public speaking and in writing speeches which also helped me to write essays. These are very important skills to have especially if you want to win scholarships. It will help you in both interviews (the ability to speak well in public) and in preparing essays.

Optimist International Essay Contest

Optimist International Headquarters
4494 Lindell Boulevard
St. Louis, MO 63108
(800) 500-8130 or (314) 371-6000
Email: programs@optimist.org
Website: http://www.optimist.org (click on *Home\Members\Scholarship Contests*)

Additional Information: This is a multi-level essay writing contest. Student winners at the district and international level win scholarships. Contestants must be no more than 19 years of age at the time of contest entry. Contest is open to citizens of the US,

Senior Year Head Start

Canada and the Caribbean. You must enter the contest through your local Optimist Club. To get contact information for your local Optimist club, visit the website for more details.

Princeton Prize in Race Relations

(609) 258-7780 or (800) 742-1036
Website: https://pprize.princeton.edu/
Social Media: Follow the Princeton Prize in Race Relations on Facebook (https://www.facebook.com/PrincetonPrize) and Twitter (@Princeton_Prize)
Additional Information: The program recognizes and rewards high school students who have had a significant positive effect on race relations in their schools or communities through their volunteer activities. Students can win a $1,000 cash prize. See website for details and to learn about previous recipients.

Profile in Courage Essay Contest

Columbia Point
Boston, MA 02125
Website: www.jfklibrary.org (see *Education \ Profile in Courage Essay Contest*)
Additional Information: In recognition of one of President Kennedy's most important legacies, this contest is designed to promote the involvement of young people in the civic life of their country. High

school students in the 9th through 12th grades can participate in this essay contest, by writing a compelling 1000 word (maximum) essay and citing at least five sources on the meaning of political courage. Registration forms must be submitted with the essay and are available on the website. The first place winner and the nominating teacher will be invited to receive awards at the Kennedy Library in Boston. Awards range from $500 to $10,000. The contest deadline is usually in early January of each year.

Project Yellow Light Scholarship/Hunter Garner Scholarship

Attention: Julie Garner
One Shockoe Plaza
Richmond, VA 23219-4132
(804) 698-8203
Website: http://projectyellowlight.com
Additional Information: High school and college students who want to encourage fellow students to develop safe driving habits can enter the Project Yellow Light scholarship competition. Your entry, which will consist of a video, billboard design or radio spot designed to motivate, persuade, and encourage your peers not to drive distracted, can win you up to $5,000 for your education. The winning video may be turned into an Ad Council

Senior Year Head Start

PSA that will be distributed nationally to 1,600 TV stations. The winning billboard design may be displayed on Clear Channel Outdoor digital billboards across the U.S. and the winning radio spot could be shared on iHeartRadio's national network. Visit the website for additional details and requirements.

The Prudential Spirit of Community Awards

Website: http://spirit.prudential.com
Additional Information: This program, sponsored by Prudential in partnership with the National Association of Secondary School Principals (NASSP), recognizes students in grades 5 – 12 who have demonstrated exemplary community service. Local honorees are selected at participating schools and organizations in November, and from these winners, two state honorees are chosen from each state and the District of Columbia. State honorees receive an award of $1,000, an engraved silver medallion, and an all-expenses-paid trip to Washington, D.C. National honorees receive an additional award of $5,000, an engraved gold medallion, a crystal trophy for their school or organization and a $5,000 grant from The Prudential Foundation for a non-profit, charitable organization of their choice. Although this program is not officially a scholarship, the funds you win, if you're an avid volunteer, could add nicely to the

1 – Scholarship Programs for Young Students

money in your college fund to pay for your educational expenses.

The Scholastic Art & Writing Awards

557 Broadway
New York, NY 10012
Website: http://www.scholastic.com/artandwriting or http://www.artandwriting.org
Additional Information: This program is designed to recognize outstanding talent among students in the visual arts and creative writing. Students submit individual works as well as art portfolios and writing portfolios for this competition. Check the website for entry details in the fall. Awards range from $500 to $10,000.

Sodexo Foundation

Stephen J. Brady STOP Hunger Scholarships
9801 Washingtonian Blvd.
Gaithersburg, MD 20878
Website:://us.stop-hunger.org/home.html or http://www.sodexofoundation.org (see *Grants and Scholarships*)
Additional Information: Stephen J. Brady STOP Hunger Scholarships are open to students in kindergarten through graduate school who are enrolled in an accredited educational institution in the United States. The scholarships are available to students who have performed unpaid volunteer

services impacting hunger in a community within the United States at least within the last 12 months. Additional consideration is given to students working to fight childhood hunger. A Community Service Recommendation is required for this application form so ask recommenders (who must not be family members) for their recommendations early. For more on requesting recommendations, see chapter 13, "The Art of Getting Good Recommendations & Requesting Nominations" in *Winning Scholarships for College* (5th edition).

Sons of the American Revolution Joseph S. Rumbaugh Historical Oration Contest

Website: https://www.sar.org/education/youth-contests-and-awards or https://www.sar.org (see *Education*)

Additional Information: Oratory competition for high school freshmen, sophomores, juniors, and seniors who submit an original 5 to 6-minute oration on a personality, event, or document of the American Revolutionary War and how it relates to the U.S. today. Oration must be delivered from memory without props or charts. For more information and complete rules, visit the website. Awards range from $200 to $3,000.

1 – Scholarship Programs for Young Students

"Stuck at Prom" Contest

Website: http://www.stuckatprom.com
Additional Information: Contest is open to U.S. citizens who are high school or home-schooled students at least fourteen years of age who attend a high school prom in the spring wearing complete attire or accessories made from Duck-brand duct tape. Entrants must enter the "Dress" or "Tux" category and submit a color photograph with their entry form and other required documentation. Winners will be selected based on a variety of criteria, including originality, workmanship, use of Duck tape, use of colors, and creative use of accessories. Award amounts range from $100 to $10,000. Contest begins in early April and ends in early July.

U.S. Senate Youth Program

The Hearst Foundations
90 New Montgomery Street, Suite 1212
San Francisco, CA 94105-4504
(800)841-7048 ext. 4540 or (415) 908-4540
E-mail: ussyp@hearstfdn.org
Website: https://ussenateyouth.org

Additional Information: Open to high school juniors or seniors holding a student office. Students must be currently elected to one of the following offices: student body president, vice president, secretary, or treasurer; class president, vice president, secretary, or treasurer; student council representative; or student representative to district, regional, or state-level civic organization. For an application contact your high school principal or state education administrator. Visit the website to find more information about your state's education administrator and the program details. The organization's advice to interested students is to apply in your junior year so that you will have two years of eligibility, rather than one year if you apply as a senior. Award is a $10,000 college scholarship and an all-expense-paid trip to Washington, DC to experience national government in action. Visit the website at the beginning of your junior or senior year for additional details and current deadlines.

Veterans of Foreign Wars of the United States Voice of Democracy Annual Audio Essay Contest

Voice of Democracy Annual Audio Essay Contest
(816) 756-3390 ext. 6155
E-mail: youthscholarships@vfw.org
Website: http://www.vfw.org (click on *Community Programs\Youth and Education*)
Additional Information: This scholarship contest is open to grade 9 through 12 students who write and record a three- to five-minute essay addressing the assigned theme, which changes each year. Previous

1 – Scholarship Programs for Young Students

assigned themes have been "I'm Optimistic About Our Nation's Future," "Freedom's Obligation," "Reaching Out to America's Future," and "What Price Freedom?" To participate in this contest, visit the website for more information, speak with your high school counselor, or contact your local VFW post. Scholarship awards range from $1,000 to $30,000. Submissions should go to your local VFW post. E-mail or visit the website to find your local post.

.

2

Can Graduating from High School Early Affect Your Scholarship Chances?

One of the questions I have been getting in recent years is whether students should graduate in the 11th grade if they have earned enough credits to do so. My answer: It depends. If you are still hoping to enter and win some of the most competitive scholarship competitions, then losing an additional year of community service, extracurricular activities, and leadership experience could hurt your chances. However, if you've packed an impressive amount of activities into an already outstanding résumé, you could be okay. Really, you never know, because there is no guarantee with scholarship competitions. You can never know the résumés of students you are competing against. And you don't know other factors that could be under consideration when determining winners. Furthermore, if your parents are saving to help you with college, your early graduation reduces the number of years they have available to continue saving. It may force them to start spending for your education before they're fully ready. Or your need

Senior Year Head Start

for college funds early could interfere with money they need for an older brother or sister already in college. Of course, if they can pay for your freshman year before facing yearly tuition increases that many institutions have, your early graduation may not be so bad. They might even consider it a freshman-year bargain.

3

Are Scholarships Available for Private School?

This is also a popular question I have been asked for many years. Finally, I have an answer. Some of the awards included in this resource are given to the students immediately as a cash prize. In this case, the funding can be used for private school. There are also a few scholarship programs such as the *Children's Scholarship Fund* that are designed to help pay the tuition for students at private schools.

You can also take a look at the Advanced Internet section in this resource. Conducting an advanced search may also help uncover private school funding in your geographic area.

4

Scholarships as a Younger Student Versus a High School Senior

There are many aspects of both searches that are the same with a few differences. The following information will explain more.

What's the Difference?

For high school seniors, scholarships may be more abundant, particularly small amounts in the community. However there may be smaller prizes and cash awards that younger students have an opportunity to win.

What's the Same?

The areas searched by high school seniors and by youth are the same. For example, your research should include books and directories in the library or a bookstore, a review of local/regional resources, as well as extensive use of the Internet. The overall process is also very similar. Once your research is completed, you should have applications which need to be completed properly and thoroughly. In addition, some scholarship applications will require essays particularly for some of the many contests open to younger students. Some may also require one or more recommendations, nominations and possibly interviews. For all, you need to highlight your activities and differentiate yourself from others who are also applying. Moreover, during the application process, you need to be very organized to stay abreast of upcoming deadlines.

5

The Search

Your search should include the following three areas:

- The library
- The Internet
- Local sources: the local search should involve searching for funds available in your community, state, and region.

For a comprehensive search that gives you the best and most opportunities to win scholarship money, devote close attention to all three!

Library Search

To start your scholarship journey, you should go to the nearest library. Once there, do the following:
- Look for scholarship directories such as the *Ultimate Scholarship Book* or *Scholarships, Grants & Prizes* from Peterson's.
- Search for books such as *Winning Scholarships for College* that go beyond the standard listing found in a scholarship directory. The focus for books of this type is to help you learn how to win scholarships. As a result, they may have limited listings but each listing would include as much additional information on winning the scholarship as possible.

Senior Year Head Start

- Search for newspaper articles about scholarships. Newspapers such as *USA Today* periodically have articles about getting money for college. To find articles in sources like these as well as the magazines above, use the library's online database or microfiche. In addition, an Internet resource you can use would be Google Alerts.

Internet Search

You can use the Internet in many ways to get college information and find the money to pay your way. The example listing in this resource gives you a general summary for many types of programs. If you're connected to the Internet and you're viewing an electronic version of this resource, you may be able to click on the underlined areas to go directly to the web pages listed for the program. If the web page you would like to view is no longer available, try an advanced search on Google because the location may have changed. Or, the competition may have been suspended or discontinued due to lack of funding or a new direction. Unfortunately this can happen at any time with any program. To help stay informed about new programs, join The Scholarship Workshop on Facebook (www.facebook.com/scholarshipworkshop) or follow us on Twitter @ScholarshipWork for information about new scholarship programs.

Advanced Internet Search

Have you ever entered a search term in the main search box and received millions of results or

5 – The Search

advertising pop-ups that really aren't relevant? An advanced search will help you cut through the clutter. You can use the advanced search function in a general search engine such as Google or Yahoo! to find specific information for your scholarship search. An advanced search helps narrow the results you might get from an Internet search.

Perhaps you want to find a scholarship for students in middle school. The example below shows the information you might include for this type of advanced search. Inputting this information into the Google Advanced search uncovered the *Davidson Fellows Scholarship* among others. You could do a similar search for "elementary" or "high school sophomores" as your exact phrases.

Advanced Search		
Find Results	all of these words	
	the exact phrase	middle school
	any of these words	scholarship
	none of these words	

Alternatively, you may want to find a community foundation in your city. If you lived in the city of Arlington, Virginia, you might include the information in the advanced search section similar to the information in the image below to find a community foundation. Conducting this advanced search uncovered the Arlington Community Foundation. The Arlington Community Foundation along with many others throughout the country maintains a list along with applications for scholarships available to students in specific communities. In your community, some of these may also be open to younger students.

Advanced Search		
Find Results	all of these words	Arlington
	the exact phrase	community foundation
	with at least one of these words	Virginia
	any of these words	

Conduct this type of search if you are looking for specific types of scholarships as well. For example, you may be interested in scholarships for culinary school. With an advanced search you might enter the exact phrase as "culinary arts," at least one of the words as "scholarships," and for all of the words, "associations." This will help you find associations that offer or administer scholarships in the field of culinary arts.

Using General Search Engines

Visit search engines such as Yahoo!, Ask, Bing, and Google. Search for terms such as, "college scholarships," "financial aid," and "scholarships." Each of these search engines will give you a list of websites and articles where the term you searched for is included. This will lead you to specific scholarship program websites.

You can also use general search engines to find out if an organization you have heard about in the news or elsewhere has a web address. For example, if a news article lists a program, put the entire name of the program into the search box of an engine with quotation marks around it. By doing this, you may be able to go directly to their website if the search engine finds a link. Or use Google Alerts (www.google.com/alerts) to get e-mail alerts for recent articles written about scholarships, college, and financial aid.

Local Search

The local search is one most often ignored by the typical student. Usually someone searching for scholarships uses a few scholarship directories and an Internet search service such as www.fastweb.com. For some students in search of college money, an Internet search service is the only resource used. Although search services similar to www.fastweb.com can be wonderful, you should not ignore other sources to find funding. If your scholarship quest includes directories and the Internet only or even just the Internet, you could be overlooking some valuable scholarship opportunities.

The best way to have a complete scholarship search is to search locally in your community, state, and region as well as using directories and the Internet. Most of the scholarships you find in directories and on the Internet are national which means that if you apply, you are among many others who hope to win the scholarship. This makes winning the scholarship harder because it is more competitive. For many local scholarships the number of applications received from students is much smaller which makes them less competitive. This is probably because local scholarships are generally smaller in monetary value and a lot of students feel they aren't worth the time and effort. Fortunately smaller, easier to win scholarships, do add up and should definitely not be ignored. In my scholarship total of more than $400,000, awards as small as $50.00 were included. And my eight year old daughter just won a small local scholarship for the area where we live.

For a local scholarship search, you should do the following.

- Search for community foundations. Visit the Northern Virginia Community Foundation (www.cfnova.org) for an example of a community foundation and to see types of scholarships a community foundation might have. Visit the Internet search section of this publication to learn how to conduct an advanced search for scholarship information.
- Research local clubs and organizations. Examples of these would be the Soroptimist Club, the Optimist Club, Exchange Clubs of America, Daughters of the American Revolution, YMCA/YWCA, the Kiwanis Club, the Rotary Club, the Lions Club, or the Knights of Columbus.

5 – The Search

Also look for sororities and fraternities. For more examples of clubs and organizations based in local communities throughout the United States, read Chapter 2 of *Winning Scholarships for College* (5th edition). Optimist International, an organization that has local clubs throughout the country, has an oratorical and an essay contest for students under age 19 where they can win up to $2500 in scholarships. I competed in the oratorical contest for the local Optimist Club in my area over 25 years ago and won quite a few awards in the process. Although I did not win the scholarship, the experience helped to develop many of the communication and writing skills that I have used successfully throughout my life.

- Contact companies and banks located in your community. Some may have scholarships available to local residents. Call the personnel or human resource department of these companies to inquire if they offer scholarships to students in the community.
- Ask your parents to check with their employers. Some employers offer scholarships to children of their employees.
- If your parents belong to a work-related union, contact the union to find out if they offer scholarships to the children of their members. Union Plus is an example of a union that maintains a scholarship program.
- Contact any organization to which you or your parents belong, local or national, to determine whether they have a scholarship program for their members. Your church or faith related organization might be an example.

Senior Year Head Start

- Since some credit unions have scholarship opportunities for their members, you should also contact your credit union, if you have one.

6

Applications

For colleges and universities, getting an application is relatively easy. For private organizations and companies, getting an application may require a little more work. However, for some large scholarship programs administered or offered by private companies and organizations, downloading applications from websites and applying online is very popular. Many students prefer applying online because it's quicker and easier. Unfortunately it's also very easy to make mistakes and to give answers, especially short essay answers, that don't reflect a lot of thought. It is also important to note that if you apply online you can't include most of the winning elements as discussed in the next chapter.

If you absolutely must use an online application, follow these guidelines:
- Print online applications first without completing them
- Complete them on paper
- Then transfer your answers from paper to your computer in the online application
- Print the completed application
- Proofread

- If you like everything and have no mistakes, press SEND or whatever button you need to press online to send the application. If you can, make a PDF copy of the applications you complete. This can make it easier to review your application to get ready for a potential interview.

For parents or guardians reading this chapter, it is very important for you to proofread and review the applications for younger students as well as high school seniors if you have them. An impressive application can help your young student's application stand out well amongst others.

7

Winning Elements

What are winning elements? Winning elements are items that set you apart from the crowd such as the following:

Your résumé/activity list

Your extracurricular activities, leadership positions, community involvement, and your being a well-rounded student are very important to winning scholarships. To show your involvement in an organized manner with a résumé or an activity list closely resembling a professional résumé helps scholarship programs and educational institutions see your participation and leadership as a whole unit rather than scattered among a few lines on an application.

Essays

Essays are also very important to your winning a scholarship. An essay is where you can really shine and tell those who read it how you feel about a particular issue. An essay can help you to elaborate on activities you've outlined in your résumé/activity list. In fact, incorporating your activities, how they have helped to make you into the student or person you are, and how these activities may have helped others, are important features to include in an essay and make its content come alive for the readers, while showing your best qualities.

Young students who need to write essays may need adult guidance. If you're an adult reading this publication for a really young student, interview him or her about their activities and help them formulate sentences to explain and showcase their activities.

Also, for some contests open to elementary and middle school students, the criteria for winning may be based entirely on an essay. These contests may also have a theme for the essay. Students who can interpret the theme well using their written words can excel in these competitions.

Samples of your work

If you have done anything extraordinary or award-winning or that has received some type of recognition, include a sample as part of your application package. For example, in my scholarship search, I included an award winning layout from the high school literary magazine where I was the editor. I also included poetry that had won awards as well. In one of my applications, I even included a poem I had written titled, "I Am a Child." I liked the poem and thought it represented my writing style and how I felt about life. It also coincided with my essay where I had written about using my journalism skills (gained through my extracurricular activities) to overcome poverty and destruction in America. The poem which had this line, "I am a child yet I have seen cruelty in the face of kindness," fit the theme of my application essay. For the essay, I had to answer the question, "You are at your 30th high school reunion. The president of the United States is part of your class. Yet, you are the guest of honor. Why?"

Make sure you don't go overboard when including samples of your work as part of your application package. One or two items you feel are appropriate are enough. Don't send anything that won't fit in a 9" X 11" envelope. And most importantly, if you are asked NOT to send anything extra, DON'T.

By the way, if you write poetry, you may be able to win a scholarship or award in the *Scholastic Art & Writing Awards* and get recognized in the *National Student Poet* program. This program is open to students in grades 9 through 11.

Articles

These articles could be on you or your activities (even if the article doesn't mention your name specifically). If you have been a part of an activity or if you started an activity that has been written about in your local newspaper or college newspaper, include a copy of the article. Once again, don't go overboard. One article, if you're also sending samples of your work is enough. Two articles should be your maximum if you're not including samples of your work.

Recommendations

(discussed in the next section)

Some programs will ask for recommendations. If they do, great! If they don't, you can still include one if it's really good. A good recommendation can help your cause even if it isn't requested by a scholarship program. An outstanding recommendation from a well-regarded individual, just like other winning elements can help to overcome a less than stellar GPA and for some programs where really young students such as those in elementary compete, winning could be based entirely on an adult's recommendation or nomination.

Résumé/Activity List

One of the best ways students can set themselves apart from others is through their extracurricular activities, especially with those that are community based. Many organizations are very impressed by students who are involved in the community and in their school or educational institution. To show your involvement in an organized and impressive way, you can include a résumé or activity list with your applications. Although most applications will ask you about your activities and include lines for you to list them, your activities look better when presented as a whole and in a résumé-like format. Some students are using the word processing wonders available today to make beautiful résumés complete with pictures and graphic elements that anyone would be proud to show in a job interview. That's the idea. It's great if you have a scholarship judge looking at your résumé/activity list and not only being impressed by what you've done but also how you presented it. Just make sure you don't overdo it with pictures and graphic elements. Content is the most important factor.

For example, you could organize your résumé in the following manner.

Departmental Clubs/Activities *Here list all activities you are involved in within your school*

- Student Council – 2018 to present *List activity and years in which you participated*
- National Beta Club – 2019 *List any positions of leadership held and year held as a subheading *
- Future Business Leaders of America – 2018 to present

Honorary Clubs * List all organizations that you have been inducted into because of outstanding performance *

- National Honors Society - 2020

Community Clubs/Service Activities
List clubs or activities within the community

- Role Models and Leaders Program – 2020 to present

Senior Year Head Start

- Macon City Volunteer Youth Coach – 2019 to present
- NAACP – 2018 to present
- Susan G. Komen Race for the Cure – 2018 to present
- Community Church Youth Group – 2019 to present

Work/Internship/Research Experience

- Laura's Babysitting Services – 2018 to present

Awards/Honors *List all the awards that you have won.*

- Volleyball Team's Most Valuable Newcomer – 2018
- Certificate of Participation – Core Advisory Day – 2020
- President's Student Service Award – 2021

*Items in italics <u>and</u> small type are notes to help you create your own résumé.

You can find other types of résumés in the 5th edition of *Winning Scholarships for College*. Different formats are acceptable as long as your résumé is easily readable and well-presented.

Recommendations

Another area where students can stand out from the crowd is through the recommendations of others. In order to get the best recommendations you need to be careful about who you ask, how you ask, and when you ask. Here are a few tools to help you do that.

7 – Winning Elements

First, consider the scholarship you are applying for. Even if the program is not requesting a recommendation, include one anyway especially if the recommendation is a good one or it highlights your community involvement. Nearly all scholarship programs are impressed by those with community involvement. If the program is requesting a recommendation, try to get at least one from an individual that fits the nature of the scholarship. For example, if it's for a STEM (Science, Technology, Engineering and Math) type of scholarship, get your physics, chemistry or another teacher in a related field to write one.

In general, you should get recommendations from the following if you can:
- a teacher
- a counselor or administrator
- a coordinator for a community based activity
- your minister or another clergyman if you have one
- anyone other than a relative who can discuss your most impressive qualities in a written format.

As you think of people to include on your recommendation resource list, make sure to include a sentence about they how they know of you. This will help you to pick and choose individuals to write recommendations as you begin applying for multiple scholarships. Also when pondering who you should ask, think about whether the person is accustomed to writing recommendations for students or if they might be a good writer. If they have never written a recommendation and/or they aren't a good writer, your recommendation could be a nightmare or a "one liner."

When you ask for a recommendation, do the following:
- Give a written description of the scholarship and/or program
- Include your résumé and any extras you plan to send with your scholarship application
- Include a self-addressed stamped envelope with two stamps (if the recommendation needs to be sent in the U.S. mail)
- Ask at least four weeks before deadline
- Follow-up to see how they are doing or if they need additional information
- Send thank you notes. You may have to ask again.
- *Winning Scholarships for College* (5th edition) includes a sample letter requesting a recommendation as well as an example recommendation chart to help you keep track of recommendations and their due dates.

8

The Essay

For most essays you can use the following five paragraph format particularly if writing is difficult for you. If writing is one of your strengths, there is no need to follow the five paragraph format. Just make sure your essay is interesting and includes details about your extracurricular activities and/or your life.

I. INTRODUCTION - ONE PARAGRAPH

- Use a quotation, poem, thought, amazing fact, idea, question, or simple statement to draw your reader into your topic.
- The main idea does not have to be stated in the first sentence, but it should definitely lead to and be related to your main idea or thesis statement, which should introduce three main points you will develop in the body of your essay.
- Avoid using statements such as, "I am going to talk about . . . " or "This essay is about . . ."

II. BODY - THREE PARAGRAPHS

- Support the main idea with facts, thoughts, ideas, published poetry, quotes, and other intriguing, insightful material that will captivate your audience.

- Present clear images.
- If necessary, use a thesaurus to ensure that you are not using the same words repeatedly. Using a word over and over will become monotonous for your audience and distract them from your subject.

III. CONCLUSION - ONE PARAGRAPH

- Restate the main idea in an original way.
- You can again use a poem or quotation to leave an impression. However, avoid using this tactic in all three parts of the essay. It may appear repetitious and unoriginal.
- Refer to the future in terms of your plans pertaining to the subject of your essay. For example, in an essay describing your future career goals, refer to yourself in the career that you have outlined. This reference should project you, and the ideas you presented in the essay, into the future.

* Special Note - Using quotations or poems can show that you are well read. If your essay looks like a dumping ground for quotes and the words of another, using quotations and poems could show something else entirely. Be selective and look for quotes that are enlightening and profound.

As you become more experienced with writing essays you can expand on the format by including more paragraphs or even reducing the number of paragraphs and abandoning the format. If you start with the basic five paragraph format, it is easy to adapt and change to fit the style of your essay, as I did when I wrote an essay for the Coca-

8 – The Essay

Cola scholarship which had nine paragraphs. I also changed the format to write an essay that had only two paragraphs. You can read both essays and an analysis of each in Chapter 11 of *Winning Scholarships for College*.

Early in your scholarship search prepare two basic essays following the format above. The essays can easily be tailored later to fit most scholarship application essay requirements. Since many essays require descriptions of you and your future career goals, let's follow the format to write an essay about you; featuring your activities. In nearly all of the essays I wrote to win scholarships, I incorporated information about specific activities in which I was involved. Once you finish, this essay and parts of it (recycling) can probably be used for every essay you write regardless of the question.

If you have an essay you need to write for a scholarship immediately, it will help if you do the following activities first.

- Finish your résumé/activity list if you haven't already. This needs to be done before you begin any essay. Using the information from your résumé/activity list, you should include additional details about your activities to support the main points of your essay. Scholarship organizations are very impressed by students who are involved in various endeavors beyond typical classroom work. Showing your passion and commitment to certain activities

by including more information about your involvement will help you stand out from the crowd of other applicants. Refer to the chapter, "Grades Don't Mean Everything," in *Winning Scholarships for College* for more information and also the "Winning Elements" section in this publication.
- Research the organization or company sponsoring the scholarship or award.
- Learn why the scholarship was established and the mission of the organization. If one or more of your activities fit the reasoning behind why the scholarship was established or the organization's mission you may want to highlight this in your essay.
- Understand the question. Think of several ways you might answer and write them down.
- Look at the scholarship application. What do most of the questions focus on: academics, community involvement, etc.? If an organization asks most of its application questions about community involvement, then try to build your essay around activities you do that benefit the community.

Since you are writing a descriptive essay about you or your future career goals, featuring your activities, the next step is to think of three adjectives that describe you. For each adjective, write down an activity that fits with that adjective.

For example, the five paragraph essay format would now look like the following:

I. INTRODUCTION - ONE PARAGRAPH
    A. Adjective/Noun 1
    B. Adjective/Noun 2
    C. Adjective/Noun 3

II. BODY - THREE PARAGRAPHS
  A. Adjective/Noun 1
      1. Activity 1
      2. Activity 2
      3. Activity 3

  B. Adjective/Noun 2
      1. Activity 1
      2. Activity 2
      3. Activity 3

  C. Adjective/Noun 3
      1. Activity 1
      2. Activity 2
      3. Activity 3

Note: You do not need three activities for each. If you have only two, that's okay.

III. CONCLUSION - ONE PARAGRAPH
    A. Summarize your adjectives and how they relate to you and your activities. Refer to the future.

Senior Year Head Start

As you write about activities in your essay, don't just list them as you did with your résumé/activity list. If you do, the essay is really saying nothing more than you already did. When you write about your activities, you should be answering these questions as part of your essay:
1. What is the activity?
2. Who does the activity benefit?
3. When do you participate in this activity?
4. Where do you participate in this activity?
5. How does this activity benefit you or others?
6. Why are you involved in the activity?

Based on the outline, adjectives, activities, and answers to the above questions, you could begin your essay like the example below, assuming the adjectives you chose were self-motivated, energetic, and compassionate:

When I think of the words self-motivated, energetic, and compassionate, I think of myself. For the past seven years, starting in elementary, into middle school and now my first two years in high school, I have participated in many activities that reflect these words. More than just words, they really describe who I am and how I feel about life.

For example, in terms of self-motivation, I built a website and Facebook page for students interested in getting tutors at our middle school and continued maintaining it during high school. Building the website and populating it with insightful content was a frustrating and challenging task I set for myself. It took me most of the summer before my freshman year at XYZ High School, but I finished it to the

8 – The Essay

amazement of my parents and friends. The website, once completed, became a much-needed reference for students in our community to find tutors and other information to help them in all types of subjects. The website also helped the upper-class students who became tutors make a little money to get a jump-start on college expenses. Most importantly, for those who weren't interested in charging, the site helped those who just wanted to aid their peers and apply principles they learned in class.

As a freshman at XYZ High School, I began to show more of my energetic traits by participating in several athletic activities concurrently which really challenged my self-motivation and determination, but most importantly helped me to relearn the value of teamwork and cooperation for all endeavors. I joined the volleyball team. I became a university cheerleader . . .

The next paragraph would focus on compassionate. The last paragraph would be a summary and conclusion. This essay is an example of a rough draft for a descriptive essay using the adjectives self-motivated, energetic, and compassionate. It still needs work but it's meant to give you an idea of how to structure your essay using the adjectives or nouns you selected and the examples of your activities that could fit the adjectives or nouns you selected.

To get additional information about planning your essays, choosing adjectives, writing about your activities, and writing different types of essays, read *The Scholarship & College Essay Planning Kit*.

9

Application Checklist

Use the following checklist to make sure you've done all you need to do as you receive new applications and send out completed ones.
1. All applications should be typed, no exceptions — unless the application requests that you print. If so, use black ink.
2. Make photocopies of applications as you receive them or download them as PDF's to a folder on your computer. To avoid mistakes in the future, complete the applications well ahead of the deadline. Also make a list of frequently asked questions and their answers. Always keep a copy of your completed applications. You may need them to prepare for interviews.
3. Set up a file system for all copies of applications so you can locate them easily as deadlines draw near. A file system is also helpful because you can refer to an application for information to use on another one. Electronic file folders using Windows Explorer are great as well.
4. All sections of the application that you are not directly responsible for should be given to those who are responsible for them as

9 – Application Checklist

   soon as possible. Recommendation forms for counselors, advisors and administrators are some examples. This is especially important when completing online applications. It is very easy to forget the sections others need to complete for you.

5. If you apply for a scholarship online, print the application first. Complete it. Then complete the application online. Print it again and proofread before you hit the SEND button. It is very easy to make mistakes on electronic applications.

6. Include your personal résumé/activity list. Most applications have space for you to list your activities and special awards, but it looks more professional to include a résumé. Never leave the spaces for this information blank. Instead, type instructions to see additional information on a separate sheet. The separate sheet will be your résumé.

7. Type essays and other supporting material on good quality paper. Use paper with a weight of at least 24 lb.

8. With your application include articles that may have appeared in your local newspaper about you or your activities.

9. Include samples of your work that are extraordinary, or award-winning. Don't be afraid to send along copies of poetry, artwork, or audio recordings of your special talents, which may include singing or dancing or playing the piano. If you have any special talent or hobby, flaunt it. It makes your application stand out from

others. When you include extra information, make sure it really is outstanding or extraordinary. And don't overload your application with extra material. Include no more than one or two examples of outstanding work. If possible, try to make sure that all of your material will fit into a 9" X 12" envelope. Most importantly, if a scholarship program or college/university requests that you not include additional information, don't. And please be aware, sending additional paper based information is usually better than sending something such as a CD. Scholarship committees usually don't have an opportunity to stop reading applications to pop in a musical compilation unless music is the basis of the competition. For some competitions, a YouTube video may be appropriate or even required.

10. Some programs that issue applications specifically request that additional pages be kept to a minimum if they are allowed at all. Respect their wishes.

11. For questions that do not apply to you, write "not applicable" in the answer blank, or abbreviated "NA," to show that you have not overlooked the question.

12. Make a recommendations list. You may be required to list the names and addresses of your references on your application. Some scholarship programs ask for this so that they can send recommendation forms to

9 –Application Checklist

these individuals directly, without using the student as a medium.

10

Keys to Preparing for College in High School

To get the best preparation for college in high school, you should focus on the following areas:

- Learn how to manage time wisely and avoid procrastination–This is one of the biggest pitfalls for college students. There are so many distractions and activities other than classes for a college student that managing time and staying on top of coursework will be incredibly difficult if you succumb to procrastination and don't manage your time wisely.
- Develop reading skills–In college, being able to get through several chapters in a book quickly and with comprehension will be very important.
- Hone your writing skills–Learning to get beyond writer's block and write well is important not only in college but also for winning scholarships to attend or finish college.
- Improve study skills–Excelling in classes will really depend on how well you can understand and retain information.
- Get involved in extracurricular activities– Colleges and scholarship programs are very interested in your activities beyond the

10 –Keys to Preparing for College in High School

classroom which help to differentiate you from others who may have similar grades and test scores.

- Immerse yourself in community service–Colleges and scholarship programs are interested in students who are committed to volunteer service and making a contribution to society.
- Explore interesting hobbies–College and scholarship programs look at well-rounded students. Selection committees and admissions officials are very interested in how you spend your time outside of high school.
- Participate in college tours–Visit colleges early. The largest and most competitive colleges and universities have the earliest deadlines for admissions and scholarship consideration. As a result, you need to know early in your senior year to which schools you're interested in applying.
- Enhance test taking skills–Most colleges and universities require an SAT or an ACT score report. Get prepared for these tests but also learn general test-taking skills so you can do well on final exams and mid-terms in college.
- Résumé writing and interview skills–For some scholarship programs you may need to interview or submit a résumé highlighting your activities. Not only that, these skills will be necessary in college as you prepare for internships, research, jobs, and other opportunities.
- Develop leadership skills–Scholarship programs and college campuses love student leaders.

Attend seminars. Volunteer for leadership positions and initiate activities to develop and showcase your leadership capabilities.
- Identify strengths and weaknesses now–If you know how to recognize your strengths and weakness, you can create a plan of action for taking remedial courses, visiting study labs, and joining study groups in college.
- Clean up your social media life. If your name and information is on a Facebook page, Twitter account, or YouTube video with derogatory, unflattering or inflammatory remarks, clean it up. Although many outside scholarship programs may not have the time to look you up on social media, there are some programs that might AND there are many universities and colleges that will, particularly if they are considering whether to admit you and/or award one of the most prestigious scholarships they have to you.
- Get prepared for the scholarship search and application process early–The most competitive scholarship programs will have deadlines early in your senior year; for example in the months of October and November. To give yourself the best opportunity to win merit or need-based scholarships, you should start preparing as early as freshman year. Researching available scholarships, yearly deadlines, and the scholarship application process well before senior year will lessen some of the pressure to get everything done and allow you to fully enjoy your final year of high school. Also, you may be able to apply for scholarship and award

10 –Keys to Preparing for College in High School

programs such as the Stephen J. Brady Stop Hunger Scholarships or Voice of Democracy Annual Audio Essay Contest, before you become a high school senior. See *Winning Scholarships for College* (5th edition) for more information about scholarships you can win from kindergarten to 11th grade. Also consider *The Scholarship Monthly Planner* from http://www.scholarshipworkshop.com to help you keep track of deadlines.

- Consider dual enrollment (if your high school offers it) or taking community college courses—Not only does this look great on your high school transcript, it can also help you when it comes to consideration for competitive scholarship competitions.
- Take Advanced Placement (AP), honors and other challenging courses—Doing so can help you prepare for collegiate level coursework. Also, certain scores on the AP exam can exempt you from taking some courses while at college.
- Become savvy with social media and online interviews. You could have a college or scholarship interview via Twitter (see Twitterviews), Google Hangouts, or some other online or social media platform.

APPENDIX

Other Resources from Marianne Ragins

Books and Publications

The Scholarship & College Essay Planning Kit
- If you have trouble getting beyond a blank page when it comes to writing an essay, this resource is for you.

Get Money for College – An Audio Series
- If you don't have time to read a book or attend a class but you do have time to listen, this audio series can help you learn how to find and win scholarships for college.

10 Steps for Using the Internet in Your Scholarship Search
- This is a resource designed to be used at your computer to walk you step by step through using the Internet for your scholarship search. It keeps you from being overwhelmed by the massive amount of sometimes misleading information found on the web. This resource is updated yearly.

The Scholarship Monthly Planning Calendar
- This convenient and easy to use monthly planning calendar will help you with time management, getting organized, and staying on

track with activities to meet major scholarship and award deadlines. This resource is updated yearly.

Winning Scholarships for College
- In *Winning Scholarships for College*, Marianne Ragins, the winner of more than $400,000 in scholarship funds, proves that it`s not always the students with the best grades or the highest SAT scores who win scholarships. Whether you are in high school, returning to or currently enrolled in college, or planning to study abroad, this easy to follow college scholarship guide will show you the path to scholarship success. One of the most comprehensive books on winning scholarships and written by a successful scholarship recipient, it reveals where and how to search for funds, and walks you step by step through the scholarship application process.

Last Minute College Financing Guide
- If you've got the acceptance letter, but are still wondering how to pay the tuition bill because you haven't yet started searching for college money, this resource is for you!

Workshops & Boot Camps

The Scholarship Workshop Presentation
- In The Scholarship Workshop presentation which is a 1, 2, or 3 hour interactive seminar, speaker Marianne Ragins proves that it is not always the student with the best grades or the highest SAT scores who wins scholarships. Instead she shows students of all ages that most

scholarships are awarded to students who exhibit the best preparation. By attending The Scholarship Workshop presentation, a student will be well prepared to meet the challenge of finding and winning scholarships. The presentation is designed to help students conduct a successful scholarship search from the research involved in finding scholarship money to the scholarship essays, scholarship interview tips and strategies involved in winning them. This presentation is usually sponsored by various organizations and individuals usually attend at no cost. Attendees of the presentation become eligible for the Ragins/Braswell National scholarship sponsored by Marianne. If you or your organization is interested in sponsoring a workshop or motivational presentation with Marianne Ragins, visit www.scholarshipworkshop.com.

The Scholarship Workshop Weekend Boot Camp
- This is an expanded version of The Scholarship Workshop presentation – It is a full day and a half of activities designed to help students and parents leave the weekend with scholarship essays, résumés, and applications completed and ready to go. The workshop weekend boot camp is usually sponsored by various organizations and individuals usually attend at no cost. Attendees of the presentation become eligible for the Ragins/Braswell National scholarship sponsored by Marianne. If you or your organization is interested in sponsoring a workshop or motivational presentation with

Appendix

Marianne Ragins, visit www.scholarshipworkshop.com.

Webinars & Online Classes

- *The Scholarship Class for High School Students and Their Parents*

- *Scholarship, Fellowship & Grant Information Session for Students Already in College, Returning to College, and Pursuing Graduate School*
    - The above classes are webinar versions of the Scholarship Workshop presentation. It is offered for those who do not live in an area where a workshop is being sponsored. Attendees of either class become eligible for the Ragins/Braswell National Scholarship.

- *Writing Scholarship & College Essays for the Uneasy Student Writer* – A Webinar

For more information about webinars and online classes available, visit www.scholarshipworkshop.com and see online classes.

About the Author

In her senior year of high school, Marianne Ragins won over $400,000 in scholarships for college. As perhaps the first student ever to amass nearly half a million dollars in scholarship money, she has been featured in many publications including *USA Today, People, Ebony*, *Newsweek, Money, Essence, Family Money, Black Enterprise* and on the cover of *Parade*. She has also made hundreds of radio and television appearances on shows such as "Good Morning America," "The Home Show," and the "Mike & Maty Show."

Marianne Ragins received a master of business administration (MBA) from George Washington University in Washington, DC and a bachelor of science (BS) degree in business administration from Florida Agricultural and Mechanical University in Tallahassee, Florida. Both degrees were entirely funded by scholarships and other free aid.

Marianne Ragins is also the author of the highly successful *Winning Scholarships for College: An Insider's Guide* and many other publications. She is an experienced motivational speaker and lecturer who has traveled nationally and internationally conducting The Scholarship Workshop presentation and giving other motivational seminars and speeches. Marianne is the publisher of www.scholarshipworkshop.com, a scholarship and college information site, and sponsor of the *Leading the Future II* and *Ragins Braswell National Scholarships*.

Contact Marianne Ragins using any of the following sources:

Appendix

- www.scholarshipworkshop.com
- www.facebook.com/scholarshipworkshop
- www.twitter.com/ScholarshipWork

www.ingramcontent.com/pod-product-compliance
Lightning Source LLC
Chambersburg PA
CBHW050604300426
44112CB00013B/2071